Dorsey

The Actual World

Other books by Erica Funkhouser

Natural Affinities

Sure Shot and Other Poems

The
ACTUAL
WORLD

ERICA FUNKHOUSER

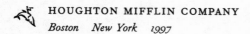 HOUGHTON MIFFLIN COMPANY
Boston   New York   1997

For information about permission to reproduce selections from
this book, write to Permissions, Houghton Mifflin Company,
215 Park Avenue South, New York, New York 10003.

Library of Congress Cataloging-in-Publication Data
Funkhouser, Erica.
    The actual world / Erica Funkhouser.
       p.   cm.
    ISBN 0-395-87707-5
    I. Title.
    PS3556.U63A64   1997
    811'.54 — dc21   97-18298
                         CIP

Printed in the United States of America

QUM 10 9 8 7 6 5 4 3 2 1

Book design by Melodie Wertelet

Grateful acknowledgment is made to the editors of the following publications
in which these poems first appeared: *The American Voice:* "Secular Garden-
ing," "Striper," "Weave." *The Atlantic Monthly:* "The Accident," "India Cot-
ton Shirt." *Compass Rose:* "Pruning." *Pleiades Artsnorth:* "Weeping Cherry."

An earlier version of "City of Windows" received the 1995 George Bogin
Memorial Award from the Poetry Society of America.

The author wishes to thank the MacDowell Colony for its generous support
and the staff of the Essex Shipbuilding Museum in Essex, Massachusetts, for
their assistance. The italicized words and phrases in "Apprenticeship" come
from an original document in the museum.

For my mother, my sister, and my brothers,
and in memory of my father

CONTENTS

I. October Farm

Saucer Magnolia *3*
The Sanctuary *5*
Salt Blocks *6*
Raspberries *7*
Midden *9*
Woodshed *10*
The Hen House *11*
Shed *14*
Cellarhole *16*
Hayloft *17*
Abandonment *19*
The Hungarians *21*
    1. 1956
    2. The Winter of the Refugees
    3. Mushrooms

II. City of Windows

1. The Window *29*
2. The Boy *32*
3. The Boy's Mother *34*
4. The Log *37*
5. Statue of the Well-Decorated General *40*
6. The Dog *42*
7. The Fountain *44*
8. The Woman *46*
9. The Gargoyle *50*
10. The Window *53*

III. The Actual World

The First Things to Come
    Up in Spring 59
Striper 60
Look at the Maple 62
The Accident 63
Aubade 65
The Bathers 67
In the Field 69
Secular Gardening 72
Pruning 74
Weeping Cherry 75
Weave 77
Some Questions 79
Apprenticeship 80
India Cotton Shirt 82
Fire Road 84

I

October Farm

Look again, and you'll see the two sisters
spooning mud into open flowerheads.

A ritual competition: who will invent
the best stuffing for magnolia blossoms?

Riverwater, wood shavings, baling twine,
oats, sweater wool, our own hair, spit —

we were always looking for new ingredients
to stiffen the ooze into a tea worth drinking.

We never thought of those compressed hours
as ornamental, or of the other sister

as anything less than essential.
Without her, we wouldn't have bothered

to experiment with honey and earthworms,
wouldn't have got into the habit of improving

upon one another — now angry, now gloating —
which has led to everything we know.

Overhead, hundreds of china-pink reservoirs
were open or opening, using their time wisely.

Seeing this was good practice for being grown.
We would never become one of the strangers

who wandered out from the house at dusk
to mumble unconvincing words of rapture.

They liked to wave their bitter drinks at us,
the ice cubes circling like carp,

but we knew none of them would bend down to enter
the purplish circumference of the magnolia

where, from every corner, hungry columns
of sugar ants hurried toward our concoctions.

Stiller water spilled over from the river
to a shallow pond;
here the sisters liked to walk
every good afternoon
to stand in the pickerelweed
until the mud had stopped bubbling
and the bullfrogs had closed
their speckled throats.

Once the croaking had stopped,
the girls could lower their hands
quickly over the green bodies.
Something in the silent afterthought to song
made the frogs still enough to capture.
As long as the frogs kept looking at the girls,
they were theirs, their clumsiness
and their longing apparently invisible.

When the cows are away
in the rocky places
that call to them like clockwork,
the sisters lie on their backs,
their heads cradled
in red depressions
left by the lapping
of long red tongues.

Midday, midsummer,
the gritty pillows are dry as rouge.
If the cows rubbed their cheeks
in these minerals,
would they bedazzle the bull?

The girls are far from the house
and the barn, far from everything
waiting to happen to them.
They doze in the hollows
left by the cows' craving for salt.

They tell a few secrets,
sculpting the reservoirs
that grow larger
each time they confide.

Two old men, father and son,
lived at the end of the road.
When we got there, they were waiting
on the porch, not really leaning
against the columns,
but not quite standing on their own.
Our mother had told us to deliver
the berries and come straight home.

The son poured water into tin cups
before we could say "No, thank you";
and the father showed us into the kitchen,
where salt and pepper windmills
made a small sky of the toaster behind.

They helped each other open a drawer
and take out a box of curled photographs.
Holding those photographs down
was the hardest thing
we had ever seen anyone do,

each picture pressed into the table,
the father's fingers on two corners,
the son's on the other two.
They looked hard at what was there,
taking a breath to explain:
the milking barn, the baptism,
Earl in his flak jacket.

Until we saw their lips tightening
to the point where they almost disappeared
into their cheeks, we had no idea
memory could be so difficult.
When they let go of the wavy white borders,
the photographs coiled up again,
suddenly, like windowshades.

We needed to leave, but we had forgotten
where the raspberries were.
Had the men put them away?
Had we forgotten to bring them in
from the porch?
Our mother would want to know
exactly how things had gone.
In the chrome sky on the table,
my face and my sister's face appeared,
wide and dumb.
I waited for her because she was older;
she waited for me because I was better
at making things up.

The blue jar that drew them here
turns out to be a salve
for tender cattle.
A momentary glint
leads to buttonhooks,
an infant shoelast,
two crimpers to fix the lids
on rootbeer bottles;
and here are the lids,
partial eclipses
against a seedling box.

Patiently the soil returns to them
its bold anachronisms;
they lift a layer of chicken wire
to unearth a leather calving glove
and a toy tractor,
its driver still gripping
the rusty wheel.

When they leave this farm,
what will they leave behind?
Will it make its way
back to the surface
in pieces, a shattered jug,
or will it keep its shape,
like these sharp tweezers
with their persistent grip
on the elusive?

✦ WOODSHED

A young girl stands at the door,
imitating a keyhole;

cordwood lies stacked floor to ceiling,
sad as anything caught sleeping.

She remembers the men splitting the logs,
hauling them here, the pungent weave of wood,

and she looks forward to the thrill
of lit logs devouring themselves in flame.

She likes to believe the wood watches her
store up what she needs for winter,

as the larvae of the bark beetle do,
inscribing the heartwood while they chew

their way toward the invisible galleries
where they will become winged.

Tonight while the others sleep she'll stake
her sheet like a nomad's tent

and prepare to wake up anywhere new
as she lights the tidy cabin of kindling

set where she most yearns for fire, in her unquiet bed,
night's emptiness stacked end to cold end.

Dusk again,
the girls follow their mother
into the valley between the barn
and the manure pile.
A few slate-blue sunflowers
rain blue seeds
on the tarpaper roof;
damp shingles curl and split.
"Last one in closes up,"
the mother reminds her youngest,
who is just coming through
the little swinging door.

Inside, the fretful hens
pace from box to box,
stitching the air around them
to the floor.
Lifting one scaly foot,
they forget to put it down.

The girls are learning
to set out the wooden eggs that trick
the hens into keeping to one nest,
or give the unimaginative ones
an idea of what might come,
or lend the grieving hens
a sort of comfort.

"Each hen's got all the eggs
she'll ever lay inside her,"
their mother says, sifting
through the slatted light
that leaves loose bracelets
in the straw.
"They're lined up smaller
and smaller the further back you go."

The older sister
has some fragile knowledge of her own.
She's told the younger one
she'll make her own eggs
in little factories
called ovaries.

They've looked through microscopes
to see how one life
might be formed inside another.
At first the chick is just a smudge;
by five days, a speck of blood,
the heart, lies caught
in a huge white sky.
Eight days: eyes vivid and blind
as burners on a stove.

While the older sister bends and sways
among the bantams with her mother,
the younger girl thumbs
her tranquil wooden egg
with its grain of islands
within islands,

hoping for some sign
of all that waits
inside her own rough chest,
of how the restless swelling
just now beginning to reach her
will one day demand to be let out.

The red shed is only a room
for shade, a cure for heat,
as buckwheat is a cure
for exhausted soil,
or card games the remedy
for a sleepless night.

On hot afternoons the horses
stand here, rump to withers,
stamping their feet
and swatting each other's ears
with vehement tails.

Not long ago,
when the sisters were ten and twelve,
they painted murals on the walls.
What would horses like to see?
Hayfields and more horses
and a molasses-colored pond.

That summer they convinced themselves
they were artistic animals.
The trees in their orchard
grew every color of apple;
their clouds bowed and reared;
they took care not to paint bridges
or frightening foxes.

Now they sneak into the shed
to light up stolen Lucky Strikes.
See? All that time
they had been perfecting
the work of the lonely.

Each day they had hurried
to adorn the rough boards,
and each day the irritated beasts
had come to the shed
as they do again this afternoon,
wanting only to close their eyes
in the shade.

✦ CELLARHOLE

They're resting between chores
as if they were human,
these board lengths
layered across sawhorses
and the wooden shutters leaning
against the stone foundation.
It's as if they had come down here
from the hayfields years ago
for a smoke and never got up.

The two sisters take in the ruin
scent by scent, from creosote
to wild mint.
They roll up their sleeves
and the hems of their dungarees.
It is time to sun themselves
on the weathered surfaces
the temperature of skin
and practice being one
with the one they love.

They begin by running their fingers
the wrong way over the wood
until they are good enough
not to get splinters.

1 *HAYLOFT*

There was no night
they couldn't imagine
in the hayloft:
nights of exploration
in clouded laboratories,
nights in the tropics
with a confusion of perfumes,
bold nights in rainy cities,
the neon letters flashing
instruction on the sidewalk . . .

The two sisters
used the trap door
in the ceiling
of the old gelding's stall;
won over with oats,
he'd let them up on his back.
They weighed almost nothing,
their desire to escape
was so complete.

Misunderstood, outraged daughters,
they were sure every mile
of cut grass and clover
was agreeing with them in the dark,
reveling in their brilliant,
unrealizable plots.
All they wanted
was to get their bodies
out of the house
so they could get started
on their lives.

In that immense silence
stacked with cubes of ripe field,
no one told them they should wait
until they knew better.
Even the haypick's
resonant question mark
lay buried in a faraway bale.

1 ABANDONMENT

We never knew what they were, those holes
in the woods behind our house.

Lined with fieldstones, their only mortar
the fists of moss coming right to the lip,

they could have been cisterns or cauldrons.
In our childish imaginations,

they stood for everything old:
more in the ground than out, full of black water.

Our mother warned us never to let ourselves down
into them, giving us the idea they were entrances

to tunnels leading to more astonishing
tunnels, like everything she forbade.

Years we spent leaning over the starless cylinders,
guessing with echoes. Measurement we wanted, certainty,

any explanation for what had once been kept there,
what searched for or given up on.

One of my brothers believed they had held a cache
of patriot muskets during the Revolutionary War;

another believed the night crawlers he let down into the dark
on silver threads would come up mouthing secrets.

My sister and I thrust offerings into the moss
and were disappointed when we found nothing had been touched.

Now, years later, learning to live
with the inexplicably wild creations

of a domestic life, or refusing to domesticate
the one thing about ourselves we hold to be deeply wild,

we go back to those stone holes.
It's possible someone dug them

for no good reason, simply because
she could no longer carry everything herself.

1. 1956

Mine was not a religious family, so when my father
arrived home on Christmas Eve with the three Hungarians,
none of us was thinking of kings.
They didn't look like kings: they were short and young
and wore clothes obviously not their own;
they looked like Elvis. My mother was sure they were thieves.

"They're heroes," my father explained. "Those thieves
the Russians have stolen their country." My father
had all five of us move out of our own
beds to make room for the strange men from Hungary.
I was seven years old; the Hungarians sounded even younger
when they said, "Birthday of our King."

"They're Catholics," said my mother. "By King
they mean Christ, the baby Jesus." I had imagined the thief
that might steal not the innumerable small treasures in my young
girl's room, but my belief in those things. My father
believed in food, chemistry, opera, and now Hungary.
My mother was devoted to some dark knot of her own.

"They've got nothing. We owe them some of our own,"
my father said. He unwrapped the packages from King's
Variety and divided my brothers' presents among the Hungarians:
plaid shirts and three black torches like the ones thieves
used in cartoons. "They lived on wild mushrooms," my father
said. "It took them months to escape. Only the young

and the desperate have the courage to leave their youth
behind in exchange for freedom." He pointed toward his own
father's atlas on the shelf; I brought it to my father;
I was still young enough to think of him as a king
as he showed me the vast forest of Russian thieves
and there, dangling like a gold ornament, Hungary,

home of these three dark strangers, the Hungarians —
Sandor, Imre, Josef, their names oddly familiar to my young
ear. Sitting in our kitchen, they didn't look like thieves
or heroes. They smoked. They were more like my own
brothers, but interested in me, these three kings
of Budapest led to our table by a star, my father.

Wary of thieves, the one named Josef slowly unfolded his own
gift, the snapshot of a young girl, her apron loaded with a king's
ransom of black Hungarian cherries, enough to save one father.

2. THE WINTER OF THE REFUGEES

Saturdays during the opera Sandor cooked.
Like a pair of trained monkeys,
my younger brother and I retrieved
ladles and stockpots, a platter
large enough to hold dozens of pigs' knuckles.

He was new to all the names —
celery, bay leaf, poppyseed —
stopping to sing a small aria
about cider vinegar, to rehearse *onion*.
He could die in any language,
and he taught us the difference between

the storefront shootout in *Gunsmoke*
and the moment when Butterfly
lifts her father's dagger to her throat.

We'd examined his forearms —
white scars like river minnows
left by miles of barbed wire.
Behind my mother's apron, Sandor
would prepare Cio-Cio-San's honorable death,
falling to the linoleum in silence,
and rising again, a splendid tree peony,
during the radio applause.

Moments later he was untying packages
of stewmeat and whacking the greens
from beets so we could scrub the roots.
Soon his friends would arrive
with mustard pickles, marinated mushrooms,
butter cookies stuffed with fig.
They gave each other haircuts,
and the women giggled as they tried on dresses
left for them by my mother's friends.

Eventually my whole family
would arrive in the kitchen.
The afternoon's coffee cups collapsed
beside the sink, and six-packs of ale
started to pile up on the counters.
There were too many of us for the table;
we sat on stools, on laps, on the floor.
The music changed to Armstrong and Fitzgerald.
We ate and ate, my family's ordinary arguments
muted by the fiercer languages
of German and Hungarian,

and the redolent language of soup being poured,
of seconds, of gravy enveloping noodles,
cabbage like a quarter-moon on every plate,
butter over pumpernickel, crisp pickles,
poppyseeds in the teeth, the church key
loosening another bottlecap.

Then began the late night language of plates pushed aside,
the polished knuckles of the pig like sections
of a tunnel to another country,
and my little brother's shy ballet
as he offered my father's contraband cigars,
the portrait of the gypsy
easy to slip off without tearing the paper,
so when we got up to dance — we always danced —
we'd all be showing off the same gold ring.

3. MUSHROOMS

My mother knew where to look.
When she entered a field,
the field seemed to want her there,
and the mushrooms that earlier in the day
had been resting underground, whispering
among themselves, poked their heads
up like hens to look for her.

I followed in her amber wake,
as did the last Hungarian, Imre,
willing to look for whatever she was looking for.
Nearly a year after he'd come to live with us,

Imre had become my mother's easiest son.
He worked for her, selling smart linen dresses
and cocktail sheaths of Thai silk.
The customers didn't dare say no
to the medal he wore around his neck —
one of the tin bells that had been dropped
from the sky over Budapest
by American planes, promising
all the free world for Hungary
in dime-store script.

We studied her casual shoulders, her easy walk,
the way she could point out a migratory warbler
and still be the first to spot
the parasol mushroom in the grass.
Our agreement was this:
I didn't have to go to school,
but I was supposed to learn Hungarian.
Often the three of us sang as we walked:
Erdő, erdő de magos a teteje
Jaj de régen lehullott a levele.
When I asked what it meant, Imre told me
all music is about love and soldiers.

Boletes, inky caps, honey mushrooms —
we found them all. When we came across Lactarius,
Imre wept over the sticky milk.
He and the others had lived on these mushrooms
and a few wild birds when they'd escaped toward Austria.
I would never have given my mother so many tears,
but Imre was the same height as she was
and let his small head fall against her shoulder.

On one of our best days, my mother found
a giant white puffball, the globe so new
it had not yet taken on any color.
How little she cared that it had no waist,
no song, that it had chosen this place,
not even a beautiful meadow,
to wait for her like a pillow.
She and Imre gave it a name: Sputnik.
On the way home they argued
whether to cook it in butter or in oil.

II ⅟

City of Windows

My mingled dread and longing now turned upon itself and
reversed its direction, so that as I gazed at an object or a face
— it did not matter which, for the choice was not mine —
I was no longer trying to establish a connexion with it, but
hoping that it — whether animate or inanimate — would
establish a connexion with me and prove to me that I existed.

— EDWIN MUIR, *An Autobiography*

The city is not mine
to organize;
that is the burden
of those who come to me,
who sit on the old wooden chair
and stare at the city
that will not respond to reason
or to prayer.

Some of the people
keep their eye on the sky,
traveling from citadel to church spire
and back again, never dropping
below roofline.
Others seek out a child
who has been sent for firewood
or try to identify the frayed wrappers
on the sidewalk — salt, candles, yeast.
Everyone turns away from the blood.

So much has passed through me,
it is hard to believe
I am still transparent,
but sunlight continues to enter;
the people of the house
return to the chair.
They rely on my simplicity:
a surface smooth to the touch,
dust that disappears
with the flick of a sleeve.

I know no words to describe
the despair on their faces.
Just as a meter has no weight,
a cloud no loudness,
the pain they carry
lacks describable properties.
What are the physical laws
of grief?, I ask myself.
How much can a window understand?

I am nothing more than glass.
Sand, soda, potash,
perhaps a bit of lime or lead
fused together in the glazier's fire.
I am the most objective
observer in the city.
Naturally I share the vanity
of those who believe they can stay detached,
who believe there is something fixed
we can call reality, if only we will ask
the appropriate questions.

Occasionally I permit myself to imagine
an inner experience
that might explain what is happening
in the city,
but I am, after all, melted sand,
a fluid posing as a solid,
and my explanations console no one,
least of all myself.

If I were given the chance
to create something of my own,
I would concentrate on the sky.
Is there no way to absorb more
of its vastness,
to be lifted and distant,
a presence that colors the sea
and gives the clouds a place to move
and be seen?

The only one who knows me at all
is the old wooden chair.
On sunlit days I leave
a changeable geometry
across the seat,
surprising myself
with pieces of light
in the shape of hastily folded letters.

They say a rat
knows its way around
after a few tries.
A maze is a maze?
Okay, but a rat
is always looking out
for other rats.
I work alone.

Another boy might pull me
into the schoolyard
to see where his brother
lost a leg;
he might want to pitch rocks
through the window of the bakery
where his uncle had been shot.
Baking the seeded rye on Wednesday,
murdered by a fellow worker on Thursday —
that's the sort of boasting
slows the others down.

I concentrate on finding a square
with sufficient exits,
a shed roof that will let me up
onto the gutters of Parliament,
where there's still copper sheathing
for the taking.
I know which footbridge remains open,
which tunnels are lit.

This morning Mother begged me
to stay home, but on my way to the door

I started up our old game,
Places in the City.
It will always distract her.
We've played it since I first learned to speak,
only now the places
aren't there anymore.

The point is to guess the location
before the description is over.
Where was the street corner
cluttered with figs?
Which cobbler kept red
high-heeled boots in his window?
I'm thinking of a clock tower
whose hour hand is missing . . .

When I had got her where I wanted her,
naming the avenues and the cross streets,
laughing and crying, the sweet aftertaste
of pastry on her tongue,
the game was over.
I fastened my jacket
and ran down to the courtyard.

I worked my way past the cemetery
up to the steep ravines.
I found the tree I was looking for.
It's not bad, my trophy.
Not bad for this winter
of never-ending snow.

As I haul it back down
to the city, my log
feels bulky as a deer behind me.
We melt the snow as we go.

It's a game, that's all.
No harm in that, is there?
A little game of remembering
the places we loved.
Small memories of small places,
all of them insignificant, really,
except that they have stayed in our heads
long after the landmarks ceased to exist.

Take, for example, the cobbler's window
with the red suede boots on display.
Ridiculous, really — tomato-red,
knee-high, high-heeled, impractical boots.
One walk in the rain and they would have been ruined.
Only young girls and rich women
wishing they were young again
would buy such foolish red boots.

The cobbler used them to tease
customers into his shop.
Once he got us inside, we were hooked.
He was a no-good flirt,
flattering us with cheap compliments
and questions about work and our families.
Even when the stitching was shoddy,
we gave him our business.
His mother had a weak heart.
We felt sorry.

I have woken up more than once
with those soft red boots
wrapped in my arms.
I could never have afforded them
when the shop was still open;
now that it is gone
I can hardly get rid of them.

Some mornings before I can get out of bed
I have to fight with the boots
to get them out of my mind.
I have to slash them and shred them
so the pieces of suede lie on the sheet
like broken tomato skins.
Only then can I get up to greet my son.

I love him so much when he brings up
something I have forgotten.
I love standing with him beside the stove,
our hands flying as the game gets going.
Speed is essential.
Neither of us likes to lose.

My son is so good.
This morning he mentioned a certain kiosk
whose attendant always smoked a cigar.
The man's belly was enormous,
and the cigar left heaps of ash
on his apron. I knew the exact location.
More than once I had smelled charred leather
as a hot ash burned its way through.

The smell of that burning apron
and the sweet dry scent of new magazines
warmed by the sunshine
were just coming back to me
when I saw my son stop to fasten his jacket.

In that instant when he closes his jacket,
the game is over.
He is no longer my playful son
but a young man who must go out
beyond the city to collect firewood,
a man who will soon be forced
to take one side or the other.

More than once I have thought about
pushing him down the stairs
to get it over with;
instead, I stand at the door
to our apartment, calling out
one or another maternal caution —
"Watch yourself, Take care,
Be sure to be home before dark."

I was a runt at the outset.
Too many neighbors,
too little sunlight.
One tree had rubbed against me
until my bark fell away,
an open invitation to beetles.
Even at the blue-green heart
of the wood, we had heard
of the war no forest would survive.
Rumors over the branches
snick-snack like squirrels.

For two winters in a row
the city has gone without fuel.
The snowfall dulls every sound
except those from the air —
shelling, artillery, surveillance.
How invisible my single stem
must have been to the pilots thinking
only of what we hide, what routes
of espionage or escape.

Well, that collective history —
one pine tree as part of a forest —
that's over now.
This morning I became a log.
The boy who worked on me
wore a thin jacket, no hat, no gloves.
I could see his whole day
had been organized around gathering me.

Before the war
his day might have been
a mixed blessing
of washing and eating,
of going to school and playing with friends,
but now all the boys
behave much like trees —
they grow as straight as they can
around the task of survival.

The boy who came after me
was like so many others —
thin, determined, a good length
of rope on his shoulder,
enough of an ax for the job.
He spit on the blade,
whetted it against his thigh;
with one hand he took hold of my trunk
as if it were the shoulder of his father,
while with the other
he chipped out the fatal wedge.

None of this took very long.
A few whacks and my bottommost branches
had been readied for kindling,
strapped to his back;
a few twists of the rope
and I was wrapped for dragging.
As an afterthought, he stooped
to collect my thin twigs.
It will be something to furnish heat
to this boy and what's left of his family.

I don't know what he is pledging to me
as he hauls me over the snow,

but I begin to know him
as I follow in his footsteps,
begin to feel sympathy for his need.
Sympathy for the boy
who has chopped me down for firewood —
what else can it be but madness?

Why else would I feel this divided ache
in my trunk, the ache of two legs
struggling against a resistant weight?
Why else would I long to cry out
when I get stuck in a mortar crater?

Is that not courtesy
I feel from the boy
as he edges me around a sharp corner?
After all, I will give off
enough heat for cooking,
perhaps even for sleep.

How I enjoy myself —
if this is not the final deception,
what is it?
I am nothing but a log, a level cut
at both my head and my foot,
a portable length
more or less equal to the height
of this boy who is pulling me
into the courtyard of his house,
keeping his eyes to the ground
to resist solicitations for kindling,
my own meager twigs
swept up so tenderly from the snow
and tucked into his pockets
as if they were pieces of bread.

5. STATUE OF THE
WELL-DECORATED GENERAL

You there, citizen
on whom youth
has apparently been wasted —
look at you, tethered to a sapling!
What state tolerates such indignity?
You've no proper uniform.
No weapon to speak of.
That ax in your fist
lacks the bite to skin a fieldmouse.

Where are your companions?
No mission could be so urgent
that a youth must be separated
from his company. Where are your leaders?
You should be learning to advance in a phalanx,
but your running is sloppy,
your eyes appear weak;
not even your breath is sufficient.

Who is defending this city?
Rebels and conquerors lurk everywhere,
behind every porch and fountain,
while you thrash through the streets
like an animal.

What are your fathers thinking?
Do they believe you will turn into a soldier
in your sleep? Do they imagine bravery
is anything less than a disciplined habit?
Where are your fathers, the soldiers?
You were born into a fighting family,
weren't you? Well, weren't you?
What? What have we here? Tears?
A boy who blubbers in public?
God help us,
we shall all be ruined.

There are so few of us left
I go out only in darkness,
crossing the street where it is narrow,
avoiding the boulevard and the park.

This scent, this one I recognize;
I have picked up on this one before.
It is the trail of the boy
who leaves by the northern gate
and takes his time in the forest.

I have traveled with him before.
He carries the faint trace
of another dog I don't recognize;
perhaps he cared for it
when there were still enough of us
to gather in packs.

He knows what a dog enjoys.
The other day, when I leaned
my full weight against his knee,
he leaned back, understanding the game.

I have succeeded in bringing him
down with me into the snow.
He pulls my front legs wide
as the handles of a wheelbarrow
and nuzzles his face against my chest.
He blows on my whiskers
until the icicles melt.
When I growl, he growls back.

Like all boys, he's playful one minute,
serious the next.
I hope I'll catch up with him.
He's something worth looking for
in this city of listless cats.

I love how he rows his fingers
the wrong way through the fur on my back,
pulling and growling and lifting his heels
as if he were the one being pleased.

Is there no time even to trample
my rubble with delight?
I suppose not.
I suppose I am nothing more to him
than verdigris and dust.

I'd like to invite the boy
to leave his log in the Square for a moment,
to stop and play on the bits and pieces
of a lost civilization.
But no, not today.
He's not amused by the idea
of racing up the Library steps
into the empty rotunda.
He hasn't the leisure to enjoy
a good howl in the roofless Museum.

If only I could speak with him . . .
If only he would come closer.
I can't possibly reach him from this distance.
I wish the young understood.
We need them to come to us,
to sit by our sides
and give us time to reflect.

I'm well aware what condition I'm in —
all my lions in ruins,
the Winged Victory lying headless
on the cobblestones.
Anyone can see I haven't carried water in years!
Without the temperament of a diplomat
I would have given up long ago.

Instead, I persevere by remembering
the old days: a recitation from Thucydides;
the *Oceanides* of Sibelius;
the great etchings of Goya
after he became deaf at fifty.
All this and more
I could share with the boy.

The honorable past —
that's what I was designed to recall.
Great moments in history are preceded
by the kind of patient conversation
for which this boy has no use.

Very well then, who am I to argue
as he hurries past,
his ax handle frozen to his hand?
I am a fountain in ruins,
memorial to failure.
Nevertheless, there's no point
in pretending that his business —
scraping by, making do, making the most
of a bad situation —
will bring him anything more grand or enduring.

A teaspoon,
one teaspoon of jam,
one each day.
I have lived like this
for a month,
for a lifetime, I forget.
I forget if I ever lived
any other way,
if it was ever easy
to pull myself up from this chair.

One spoonful a day.
Lingonberry.
Grandmother boiled the jam,
mother kept it on her shelf.
Now they are both dead,
the reports of their deaths
all that is left —
one found beside the road
where she'd gone to pick nettles,
one caught by a sniper in the line
where we all wait for water.
I was too far along to drag them home.
About my husband, missing for months,
there is not yet even a story.

And now labor begins.
Could I have done anything differently?
There are so many ways out of this world,
the city has taught us,
most of them brutal and random,
but still there is only this old way in.
Tonight or early tomorrow
I will spread my legs wide
and become an entrance
to the city of death.
I measure the minutes
lingonberry by lingonberry.

The apartment is too cold
for a baby — the glass
of the jam jar icy
as the windowpane.
I think one teaspoonful at a time —
the baby must be kept warm.
Fuel for a single night —
that's what I need.
Tomorrow is soon enough
for the baby to learn
the hard lessons of the city.
Not tonight,
not its first night on earth!

That's why I must go down
to the courtyard
and steal the log from the boy
who brings home wood every evening.
His mother, whoever she is, is lucky;
she's had him at her side
for a good ten years.
What right has she to complain?
Tomorrow she can send him out again.
Tonight I must get what I need.

This is no time to beg.
The boy with the log
will be along any minute.
I could never lay my need
out before him
like a bad hand of cards.

That's why I've wrapped
my husband's gold trumpet
in a clean linen cloth
and tucked it inside my cloak.
I will wait in the shadows.
One swipe at the back of his neck
ought to do it. I promise
no skin will be broken.
He'll never know it was me.

As I walk down the stairs
one by one, I ask myself:
Do the boy and his mother enjoy radishes?
Did they ever carry jasmine
home from the market?
I may as well be trying
to keep the whole city alive.

I'm sure I won't kill him.
The pain should be nothing more
than what I felt just now in my legs.
I'll see that he doesn't freeze.

When the news gets around,
I'll stop by with a gift of jam.
Perhaps his mother will make cocoa
and we'll talk like two mothers anywhere,
holding our children in our laps,
trading the stories of how they were born.

Sculpted to terrify,
I am truly the most pathetic sight
in the city, a gutterspout fantasy.
Even the boy passing below
doesn't bother to aim a stone
at my mossy grimace.

I tell you, so much
of the city has disappeared,
I have begun to look elsewhere
for answers.
When the building
that kept you in shadow
is shattered and falls,
letting the sunlight
land directly on your face,
you can't help but discover
greater sources of obscurity.
Look at that blasted façade,
that gaping cellarhole.
And over there, six whole stories
of splintered windows . . .

In the midst of all this
I have begun to believe
I possess a soul. A beautiful soul!
I, whose composite nature
renders me lower than moles.
Nameless and nationless,
I may as well have been copied

from a lunatic's sketchbook.
Head of a leering lion,
torso of a crayfish,
extravagant talons.

To make matters worse —
don't laugh! —
I have fallen in love
with my secret possession.
When I look down on the street
I am convinced no one there
has a soul more beautiful than my own.

We are a city at war —
what has come over me?
It would be safer to display
a dozen loaves of fresh bread
or a working car battery
than to sit here, this belief
shining across all my features,
just asking for shrapnel.

There's no hiding
my blind devotion, the commitment
to persevere.
I mewl and I whimper.
I pretend I am a reliquary of gold
in which to house my invisible beauty.
I imagine hoarding opals and bananas.
I compose a rock opera
and swear that one day my soul
shall wear velveteen slippers.

For all I know, my poor soul
is large enough to encompass
all our sad countries.
It is so beautiful and so tender.

You should see it calling to me,
opening its lavish white border.
There are no faces there,
no bodies, no architecture, no weeping;
just this white invitation,
acceptance, forgiveness.

Once again the chair is occupied.
I recognize the woman
whose boy brings home firewood.
If only I could offer
a snifter of brandy,
a woven rug for her legs.
Alas, I possess nothing more
than the transparent hour
in which she is free to remain here.

A light snow has started to fall.
In the courtyard,
the boy turns a corner with his log.
And there, in the shadows,
the dark eyes and quick movement
of something feral. A dog
or a person? A person.
Can the woman beside me
see what is there?

I know she has questions of her own.
So many months since she has heard
from her loved ones.
New armies gathering
on the outskirts of the city.
She closes her eyes.

She has been dreaming again.
I know her dream by heart now.
She is walking beside the river,
the bridges festooned in wildflowers,
the air scented with plum.

It must be somebody's wedding,
but when she gets to the riverbank
she is handed a copper platter
on which a fish lies dead
from swallowing a snake
too large to digest.

The fish and the snake lie together,
the snake's body filling
the waxen mouth of the fish.

I will forgo my usual questions.
What difference does it make
what snake? what fish? what river?
Tonight it will be better
if she leans her forehead
against the cold surface of my glass.
If she doesn't try to speak.

The hour here passes so quickly.
I've heard her say she believes
it is important to speak the unspeakable,
to make the truth travel
as quickly as gossip
and reach all the right people.
I share that conviction, believe me,
but tonight she is sad and weary,
and the shadows in the courtyard
promise nothing but pain.

Use me, I beg her.
Close your eyes, rest your head
against my dispassionate glass
and grieve. Only grieve.
I have plenty of time
and no story of my own,
not even a melody from childhood.
Fluid posing as solid,
I will hold you as long as I can.

III ᐟ
The Actual World

1 THE FIRST THINGS
TO COME UP IN SPRING

She stands above them helplessly,
her rake in her hand.
Not this year, she pleads.
Don't you see everything is different?
She is speaking to the flowers,
the dirt, the earthworms
elongated with effort.
She raises her voice to the whole season
of wracking renewal.

She'd like to still the light breeze
that grazes the back of her neck
and the change in their song
that elevates the birds in the shrubs.
She'd like to banish
the newly returned waxwings
flocked in a flurry of molten color
in the overgrown honeysuckle.

Do they think this is the same place
they stopped last year?
Do they think she came back as they did,
with a beauty guaranteeing abundance
or with the fierce armature
fit to guard a more private display?
Stop calling to me like this,
she begs the sweet earth, as she rakes
its relentless embellishments.

The boy at the end of the dock
has lent her outboard oil;
she once towed his Whaler
and held the bow line as he plucked
seaweed from his small propeller.
They know the names of each other's boats
but not each other.

This morning he's hunched
over a huge striped bass,
flicking gurry into a plastic bucket.
What looked from a distance
like frenzied skill
turns out to be a kind of suffering;
as she approaches, he's struggling not to cry.

She focuses on the fish.
The head, the tail, the cavernous guts
have already been removed;
still, the boy's arms disappear
as he works inside the fish.
He's had it weighed — fifty-two pounds,
close to a local record.

The price is good now.
As he fillets the choicest cuts,
he starts to tell her who will buy
the bass, but he stops himself
and looks away. "I was only out there
because my father died
and I didn't know what else to do."

She'd like to introduce herself.
Comfort would come more easily
if they knew what to call each other,
so she stumbles toward articulation,
imagining she could speak to this boy
about how much she misses her own son,
who left so casually, perhaps,
because his mother stays in place —
not sick, in no real danger.

The fisherman is the first
to recompose himself.
Sheathing his knife, he washes his hands
in seawater and pulls his baseball cap
back down to shade his amber eyes.
He could use some help
carrying the fish up to his cooler.

They lay the thick, translucent flesh
down on the ice, piece by porcelain piece.
When they're done, they pour the bloody scraps
into the bay. She's saying goodbye
when he says, "No, wait.
You'll want to see this."
By this he means the black crabs
clattering out from the dark
beneath the dock to feed
with delicate ferocity.

1 LOOK AT THE MAPLE

It has been standing like this for years,
big sturdy branches in tender gray skin.
She never looked out here in the moonlight before.
Tonight the maple is lathered in moonlight.
It seems to be made entirely of flesh and light.
Where it is dead and where it is living
she cannot say, but thousands of leaves
are hurrying toward the pedicels
where tomorrow they will start breaking through.
The weight of staying in place
has left vertical cracks in the trunk.
She doesn't know what kept the lower branches
from lying down in the grass;
before tonight it had never occurred to her
to come out here and support them herself.

She heard the hasty scraping of sole and heel
against the clipped turf of the doormat;
then their neighbor rushed in,
just back from the hospital,
where everything was fine, she said.
Fine. Her son had to spend the night
for observation, that was all.
He had been grazed by a delivery van
while crossing the street on his bike.
A few bruises, a superficial wound
above one knee. Incredible luck.
The neighbor was still wearing
her jogging clothes — pale blue
rip-stop nylon, the same blue flame
along the instep of her running shoes.
She slid a chair from underneath
the kitchen table and sat down,
her long legs straight in front of her
like a ladder to a different world.
It was when the neighbor answered "yes"
to a question the woman's husband
had not yet asked
that the woman finally understood.
Her husband had not even mentioned eggs,
but the neighbor knew he was going to cook.
How many times had they eaten together,
the woman watching wondered. Enough.
Her husband worked slowly,
strolling back and forth between the stove,
the coffee maker and the table,
where his wife and the still-flushed neighbor
leaned on their elbows discussing

the hazards of dusk.
On the counter, the eggs
developed little caps of moisture.
Her husband put lots of butter
in the pan and popped the toaster manually
before the toast could burn.
At long last he broke the eggs.
She had never seen him
do it like this before, two-handed.
He always liked to show off
by breaking the eggs with one hand.
This evening his hands were trembling
as he cracked the eggs
on the skillet's rim, hurrying to slide
the whole brimming mess into the pan
to quiet the sizzling fat.

She coughs, he shifts;
he sighs, she keeps
her palms crushed
between her knees.
Soon he'll rise
to boil water,
make nothing,
relight the fire.
She'll find her way
into work clothes.

On the night table
in a pink saucer,
six snake eggs
their daughter found
beneath the porch.
Once as soft
as white kid,
the eggs have split;
inside lie six
dead coils,
their red saddles
rimmed in black,
still brilliant.

Before he'd clicked
the light off,
she reminded him
only snakes
can swallow objects
larger than themselves.

Then, together,
into the mouth
of night.

Now they're late
for work, children
yet to wake,
messages blinking
on the muted machine.
Who in the world
remembers the song
for a good clean morning?

On this street,
dawn breaks;
grackle and crow
start in.

As they wash each other,
they think of the babies they have washed
and of their own parents, whose old skin
refuses the balm of warm water, preferring
to be hoisted toward a white towel and talcum.

They remember sitting in car washes
as children, the squid-red mops pressed against
the windows, wanting to get in;
and they recall the hour-old pleasures
of thumbing soil from fingerling potatoes
and unthreading the flesh of a fish from its ribs.

Her work boots, lubricated with mink oil,
wait outside the bathroom,
and his clarinet reeds are downstairs
sizzling in witch hazel.

When the rain comes, they lie back to listen
to the water replenishing the maples,
the dusty lilacs, the nearly white hearts
of the seedling lettuces in the garden.
The downpour lasts long enough
to wash the debris from between the rocks,
leaving a cleansed light in the crevices.

They are still discovering places they have missed
when the ruminating deer beneath their window
cleans the rose of its sweet buds,
and a waking owl clears its throat,

and night rises, black as a soapstone sink,
with a scoured half-moon that lets
its light spill over like chrome
onto the fur and tar and fear
of the world below.

One of them started toward the field;
the other followed: they were nothing
if not loyal.
He was searching for a shape
so pure it would both magnify
and diminish their story.
The two of them would disappear
from the troubled field
and arrive at one another's feet
in undulating beams of light.

She couldn't get over the weeds,
their flowers and wavering leaves
breaking from the stems
in magnificent arrangements.
Plantain, chicory, vetch . . .
surely they hadn't yet seen
all that was here.
If only she could discover in the purslane
a pattern that would strike him as significant,
or point out the meridian in the knotweed
where every knot comes undone.

How she longed to use what she knew,
but the life of the weeds,
their adaptive eccentricity,
seemed less brave now than foolish.
And where was her love? Walking the boundary
and begging for honesty in this,
their last day in the field.
He, at least, was consistent:
an honest detachment, an honest farewell.

She kept falling back into memory
with its thicket of unanswered questions.
Did they ever lie down in the field
when they were happy?
Did he learn anything from her
when she did what he wanted?
Did she tell him what she believed
when she was sure?

He was growing impatient,
scanning for something to leave her with
that left him not empty but free.
She, too, was thinking of gifts.
They had been kind to each other;
you could see this in their eyes,
equally heavy with trying.

If they were going to walk away
from each other over this field,
they needed to know what it contained.
One lick and the wild sorrel
comes up lemon on the tongue;
the celandine stems leave fierce
gold streaks on bare skin.
As she said this to him,
he was longing for something he could trust —
the impersonal certainty of the sky,
or a small improvement around the house
that bespeaks some faith in the future.

What he loved about success was its subtlety.
It's so easily overlooked, he observed.
She thought immediately of failure,
which reminded her of a flower
she had never been able to identify —
it had grown somewhere near here —
a putrid-smelling orchid, or nightshade.

She used to watch the bees as they entered.
They took a long time;
it wasn't till they'd started to back out
that they released the awful current
of fester and burn.
He wished he didn't have to hear any more;
he was already looking forward to the silence
that would relieve him of hunger and shame.

No, really, she said. Honestly.
I don't know why
I never showed you that flower.
You would have loved the magenta blossom
like a silk pajama button,
how it carried its own solitary radiance.

1 SECULAR GARDENING

Admitting the white bee balm has failed
in front of the hot,
south-facing clapboards
amid thriving lavender and flax,
she tears out what's left
of the black circuitry,
the rough, square, sorrowful stems.

A paradise of nodding white —
that's what she had imagined,
lacking any more precise image
of the landscape surpassing beauty
or the gates one travels through
to discover bliss.
Bliss is not a real gardening term.
There are too many variables,
too many pests and drainage problems.

If all had gone well, the bergamot
might have blossomed somewhere between
her shoulders and her chin,
inviting bees to release
the true scent of summer
as they satisfied themselves
among whorls of unapologetic white.

Now what? Something that climbs?
A trumpet vine to attract the hummingbirds?
No, she will just transplant the chives,
their tapering grass spikes
reptilian green and the flowerheads
a dry, delicious purple firework
that stays in the sky
long after the ceremony is over.

1 PRUNING

To get the shape right
one must be capricious as a twig —

crave sunlight and audience
and leave things open to the rain —

respecting, at the same time,
the solemnity of the whole tree.

Certain irrevocable decisions
must be lived with.

After a point, one sees
what one's life is going to be,

what one really knew all along.
Grace requires adaptation

to circumstance,
learning to work with one's nature,

one's form, and one's annual growth.
This and that may be fed or encouraged,

propped up or sung to.
Everything dead must go.

Whoever invented the weeping cherry?
Who had the idea to cut off
the upward flowering head
and turn it upside down
before grafting it onto the trunk
so all the branches would have to look back
at the earth from which they came
and do nothing but weep?

I planted this tree when my grandfather died.
That was years ago, my first death,
when I was still pursuing experience
rather than trying to keep out of its way.
I planted the tree myself,
filled the shade at its trunk with squill.

I think I was remembering a night I spent in Greece.
I stood on a rooftop with two friends.
We had been drinking beer and dancing
to terrible bouzouki music.
That was one of the last nights of my youth,
however little I understood its significance then,
the beautiful length of that single night in Athens.

On the roof high above the street
smelling of lamb and sawdust and anise,
we danced under a cascade of shooting stars
that lasted till the first light of dawn.
I don't know how we saw so many stars
in the middle of the city;

I can't remember if we looked up
while we were dancing or if we lay down
and did nothing but gaze at the stars.

They fell from some inconceivable height,
and they fell in continuous branches
until they almost touched the grape trellis
that lined our small rooftop.
They got bigger and brighter
the closer to earth they came.

That was how we believed our own lives
would be coming to us.
All we had to do was look up.
We were prepared to be dazed and dumbstruck.
We were prepared to be burnt.
We had no idea what we were talking about,
and that made our wisdom contagious.
We promised to remember always the sensation
of lying unafraid at the foot of a flaming tree.

That must have been the reason for the weeping cherry,
but I'm still going to dig mine up.
It doesn't belong here. It's a memory tree
flaring out of a landscape nobody sees
but myself, and when I look at it now
I know too much to enjoy it.

I see it is too close to the wall
and has nothing to do with these New England apples
and sumac and fern. The pink petticoat blossoms
look like melted sherbet, and the knot
from which the poor branches fall
is as ugly as anything I have ever seen in a tree.

1 WEAVE

Three times he returned to the woman
who designs new hair,
giving himself to her mirror,
her apron, her scissors and tissue.
She took samples from his crown,
from the more rapidly graying temples.
She gave him words for the texture,
the habit of growth.
With her fingers she described
how the new hair would be woven
together with the old,
how he would come back every few weeks
for a trim.
He had never enjoyed a tailor this much,
nor a woman. Everything she needed
she took from his hair,
the only part of his body still healthy.
When he offered photographs of himself
as a younger man, she told him
to put them away. She promised
to do something with spikes,
something defiant. After all,
this is the hair he would wear to his death.
It was true. Other people
settled their affairs privately
or said goodbye in one continuous party,
whichever generated the least pain.
He had decided to touch up his hair

the way a young boy would touch up
his favorite model airplane,
licking the brush to a fine tip,
enameling the evil eye on the cockpit
so it would never be mistaken
for a flower or a halo.

1 SOME QUESTIONS

They've cut him, bled him, sewn him, sent
liquid of every color into his sorrowful body.

If gravity is such a powerful force,
why does the grass stand up straight?

Why is there no black in daylight sky?
What makes the beautiful waves in the desert?

He took us to the sea, the mountains, new cities.
We wheel him from one ICU to the next.

The doctors straighten their name tags
and speak as if they had been wired with answers.

He was never any good at conversation himself,
but he answered our questions,

his attention to detail a kind of affection,
hard won as the garnets he made us walk miles to mine.

At least in our memories there is something hard and red;
where he is going there is nothing to grasp;

even the bridges our hands make with his
suffer from the clumsy engineering of grief.

The computer printouts are the size of pillowcases
and must be initialed every few minutes.

How does the nymph in the mud know it is time
to crawl up into its long day as a dragonfly?

✶ APPRENTICESHIP

When she signed her son over
    to Jacob Story, housewright, Chebacco Parish,

Hannah Burnham, widow, of Ipswich,
    was just learning how to bear her grief

through the lavender shadows of winter, to feel generous
    once again toward her husband's rooms, their children.

Several daughters remained; a son still sucked on her breast;
    death had knocked on every door that December —

smallpox, consumption, cradle fever —
    she'd lost less than many of her neighbors.

Still, on moonlit nights she'd let herself lie down
    under the luculent pear tree to weep.

Who can teach us how to grieve except by example?
    At least her husband had been kind enough

to let her see his sigh diminish over months
    until the silence came to both as a relief.

By the new year, Hannah had agreed to *bind out her son*
    to learn the trade, art or mystery

of building a house, *to dwell with and serve*
    his appointed master. Above all else practical,

she had learned the terms from her husband:
    trunnel auger, hollow plane, chisel,

the precision delicious on his lips
    as figures from the Bible,

Samson and Delilah of the tool chest.
    As to the mystery, who can ever guarantee?

There were thresholds in her own house
    where she still met her husband's skillful touch.

Her young man, then, she did indenture to faithful service,
    his master's *secrets* sworn to keep.

Taverns he shall not haunt or frequent;
    gaming, fornication, matrimony — all forsworn.

In exchange, at year's end, he would receive a pair of suits,
    one plain, one to wear *for Lords days.*

Promise, covenant and agree were spelled out boldly, for emphasis,
    the goat-brown backs of the letters erect, precise.

Then, three sets of hands and seals laid down, the first
    of January, 1801, the day itself

like a cart horse indentured to the month;
    the month apprenticed to the whims of winter;

the season receiving its instruction
    from a cast-iron sun severe behind the creaking spruce.

1 INDIA COTTON SHIRT

She saw it in a secondhand shop,
another woman's shirt given away
in a fury of forgetting
or refusing the imperfect fit,
and she wanted it
because of the man she imagined
taking it off of her.

They would argue a little,
one of a good love's
better arguments:
who gets to perform the small favor
that will bring both of them pleasure?
This time, he'd win;
she could already see
his flickering hands.

White embroidered on white,
the threads pulled through by a needle
so fine it left behind no tracks.
A geometrical design,
none of the limitations
of resemblance.

Every white blouse
is an expression of faith,
the immaculate clothing in which
one may regard oneself
with a little arrogance,
a little vanity.
One has finally got old enough
to see through one's own flaws.

She knew what was wrong with her;
she knew her gifts.
She tried the shirt on, not for size
but for texture.
Was it interesting enough
to come between her
and this new love who had come to her
when she had almost forgotten the unexpected
might take the shape of a man?

She could see him loosening the shirt
as he loosened his own.
Now his, now hers.
The gathered cuffs scalloped and roomy,
the delicate shell buttons
set out in threes, the button loops
softened by use.

1 FIRE ROAD

Who are these people — old man, old woman —
who've pulled their car off the highway
to park here where I like to walk?
They came for the silence, the privacy,
I imagine as I move quickly past.
The car windows are open; it's a warm day
for October; they offer no gesture
of recognition or need.

He has pushed himself back from the wheel
and slipped into her arms,
where he sleeps; at least his eyes are closed
and his half-frame glasses have been smudged
back up into his thick white hair.
She runs her hands slowly down his chest
as if through a pelt of fur.
Above them, the oaks and maples stand newly naked,
their way of preparing for winter, giving themselves
the least chance of being broken by snow.

Saturday nights, teenagers come to this spot
to swirl bourbon into lukewarm Pepsis
and practice love. They leave everything behind.
You've seen other spots like this —
on dirt roads, hidden away, used and used
like bedrooms, except that no one comes back
afterward to straighten up.

It's impossible to say whether it was his news
or hers that brought these two out here today.
Perhaps it was no news at all.
Whoever they are, I am sure
I have never given myself in sleep
as he does, letting himself down and down;
and I know I have never taken
anyone into my arms as tenderly as she does,
not growing tired of looking into closed eyes,
of running a thumb over the yellow buttons
of an old sweater vest.

If you know these people, if you are them,
believe me, I can't get you out of my mind.
I have come home to practice sitting
as you do, holding and being held.
As I write this, I am letting myself
weigh more. I welcome the weight.